D1287890

All You Need Is a Ball

What Soccer Teaches Us about Success in Life and Business

IDOWU KOYENIKAN

www.ikelevates.com

ISBN: 978-0-9906397-2-5

DEDICATION

I dedicate this book to God, through whom all things are possible; to my wife, Ashley; to my sons, Samuel and Joshua; and to my parents, Felix and Adenike Koyenikan.

CONTENTS

INTRODUCTION

The pursuit of success has long been a common theme in the lives of people around the world. The interesting thing about success is there is no set point for a person to be considered successful. Everyone has his or her own definition of what success is. For some people, success is passing an exam, becoming a schoolteacher, or earning a million dollars. In my opinion, success is achieving any worthy goal that you set for yourself.

I have spent a big part of my life learning all that I can about success. I have also pursued answers to some very important questions about success: What makes people successful? What makes businesses successful? What makes teams successful? Can the principles of success be easily taught and duplicated?

As a business consultant, I have also spent a good portion of my time teaching and coaching individuals and businesses on the principles of success. My search for a universal language through which I can teach these principles is one of the things that attracted me to the game of soccer.

Soccer is the most popular sport in the world. It is loved and played by people of different languages, cultures, and ages. The World Cup remains the single biggest sporting event in the world. As I began to look deeply into the game of soccer, I asked myself a very important question: Could certain elements in the game of soccer translate into personal success and success in the business world? From what I have gathered, the answer is yes—and there are several of them.

Soccer is like a language all its own. I wrote this book so I could communicate to people around the world in a universal language. The sheer popularity of the game means most people already know the concepts and terminology of soccer. For the purists out there, I understand the game is called "football" around the world. I refer to it as soccer in both the title and throughout the book to minimize confusion (i.e., I don't want anyone to think I'm talking about American football). With that said, I hope everyone enjoys this book and learn something from this beautiful game we all love. I wish you much success.

1 ALL YOU NEED IS A BALL

Many have sight, but few have vision.

I have spent a lot of time thinking about why soccer is the most popular sport in the world. And I finally figured out two main reasons for its widespread renown. The first is this: All you need is a ball. I will cover the second reason in another chapter. So you can better understand the idea behind "all you need is a ball," let me take you through a quick journey through my childhood.

I spent my early years in a city called Lagos. Lagos is in Nigeria, in the western part of Africa; it is home to people of all income groups, from the extremely poor to the extremely wealthy. In Nigeria, soccer as a sport trumps all other sports. Almost every day on every street corner around the city, you will see groups of people playing soccer. This is the same for majority of the countries around the world.

What I realized about soccer is this: No matter how poor you are, you have everything you need to play the game. To play most sports, you need special equipment, which is often not available to the average person. For example, in tennis, you need racquets, a special surface, and a tennis ball. For basketball, you need a basketball hoop in addition to the basketball. For baseball, you need a baseball bat, a catcher's mitt, and more. For the game of soccer, however, all you need is a ball.

In fact, you don't even need a real ball—you just need something that will do the job of a ball. Many times when I was young, my friends and I played with paper or plastic bags wrapped in tape, pieces of cloth knotted together, and anything else we could use. For the goal, we used stones, sticks, cups, shirts . . . anything, just as long as it signaled where the goal line was. We also played on all kinds of surfaces: concrete, mud, grass, sand—you name it. We were happy to play. All we needed was a ball to start a game.

Soccer is the biggest sport in the world because it is simple: All you need is a ball. When you understand this, you understand the power of simplicity. The concept I call "all you need is a ball" can be applied to everyday things.

When organizations approach me for help with certain issues, I use this same concept with them. I call it the "all you need is a ball" approach. When businesses employ it, they can streamline their processes, set up in new markets more quickly, deliver on their promises faster, achieve speedier market capitalization and market penetration, and get better results.

Individuals who also use the "all you need is a ball" approach see improvement in their lives. This approach aids in your communications, helps you build deeper relationships, and improves your time management skills. Overall, it makes you more efficient.

Take a good look at your life. What does your day look like? What type of routines do you have? How do you approach life's various challenges? If you look hard enough, you will discover areas in your life that you can simplify. When you put the power of simplicity to work, it will help you get bigger and better results in your life.

2 NOW OR NEVER

Many times in life, we are held back from achieving our goals because we do not commit ourselves wholeheartedly. With an escape route in mind, we hold ourselves back from giving our all.

At halftime in the 1987 European Cup final game between Porto of Portugal and Bayern Munich of Germany, Bayern Munich was 1-0 up, courtesy of a goal by Ludwig Kogl. In his halftime locker room talk, Coach Artur Jorge of Porto looked at a group of his players and asked them a simple question: "How old are you?" The players responded with their ages: 28, 25, and 27. The coach said to them, "This is your last chance to be truly successful and become part of footballing history. Now get back out there and play your best."

The coach's message to his players was clear: It was now or never. The Porto team went back out in the second half and won the game 2-1, with goals from Juary and Rabah Madjer. Porto's coach had successfully motivated his team to claim victory in a major European Cup final.

Fast-forward 25 years later to the 2012 Champions League season: Chelsea FC of England players included Didier Drogba, John Terry, Frank Lampard, Ashley Cole, Peter Cech, and Branislav Ivanovic, all of whom were nearing the end of their careers. This group of players formed the spine of the Chelsea team and collectively made a decision to win arguably the most important trophy in European club football.

They had come close to winning the Champions League many times before but never succeeded. This particular year seemed like the last realistic chance for them to win the coveted trophy. In the end, they overcame all odds and won a victory over Bayern Munich of Germany in the Champions League

Final—on Bayern Munich's home stadium, no less.

These two stories share a common theme: a group of players facing their last realistic chance of winning an important trophy together. It was a "now or never" moment for them, where they had to either push to get the result they wanted or forever wonder about what could have been.

The players deciding that it was a "now or never" moment did not guarantee their victory. But it gave them an added edge to improve their performance. Most athletes will tell you that sometimes this edge is the difference between success and failure.

There are times in life where you are backed into a corner, and you need an extra push to get you through hard times. Whether it is achieving a dream, a goal, or some other pursuit, your mind, when used correctly, can be an extremely powerful tool for achieving success. Your mind will believe and act on whatever information you feed it. When you say to yourself, "If I don't do this now, I will never get another chance," your mind begins to think in terms of possibilities and find ways to make that thing possible—as if success is your only option.

3 THE MOMENT OF MAGIC

If a tree's strength is judged while it is still a seed, it is mistaken as weak.

Paolo Maldini is widely regarded as one of the greatest defenders of all time. A one-club man, he spent his entire career at his club side AC Milan, in Italy, where he made his first team debut at just 16 years old. A fantastic player, he was the captain of both AC Milan and the Italian national team.

In an interview conducted in 2015, a now-retired Maldini discussed his playing days, saying his coach at the time—Arrigo Sacchi—used to ask him and his teammates to repeat drills over and over again in training. He said they repeated those drills so much that if he were to meet his old teammates, like Franco Baresi, Alessandro Costacurta, and Mauro Tassotti, again, they could still play like the did in the 1990s. He said that the way they trained stuck in his mind and it was one of the secrets of their team's success.

Think about it for a moment. How can Maldini feel like he can play as he once did several years later after retirement? Why is Cristiano Ronaldo so good at taking free kicks? The information I am about to share with you regarding the different stages of learning will show you how. It will help you understand how Maldini, Ronaldo, Messi, Hazard, Neymar, Maradona, Zidane, Pele, Beckham, and all the top players in the world became so good at what they do.

The Stages of Learning

Unconscious Incompetence

This is a stage of learning where you don't know how to do something and you don't know that you don't know. You are completely unaware that you do not have the skill.

Conscious Incompetence

This is the stage where you do not know how to do something, but you are aware that you do not know. This is a critical stage of learning because to grow and develop a skill, you must first be aware that you do not have that skill.

Conscious Competence

This is the stage where you know how to do something, but it takes a lot of concentration to get it done. You are improving at doing it, but you still must put in a lot of focus to get it done well.

Unconscious Competence

This is the final stage of learning, where you no longer need a conscious focus to display that skill. You have become so good at it from constant repetition that you can even "do it in your sleep."

Words like "genius," "phenomenon," "gifted," and "brilliant" have all been used to describe the best soccer players in the world. I have observed that all the remarkable things they do occur during a moment I call the "moment of magic." Unconscious competence, which is the final stage of learning, is what leads these players to their "moment of magic." This is the moment when a player does something special on the field that wows everyone. Some examples of some moments of magic in soccer history are:

- The moment when Ronaldo scored a long-distance strike in the Champions League game against Porto.
- The moment when Messi dribbled through Getafe's defense to score a great solo goal.
- The moment when Zidane volleyed the ball to score with his weaker left foot during a Champions League final game.
- The moment when Real Madrid fans applauded Ronaldinho after an amazing display against them.
- The moment when George Weah picked up the ball in his own box and dribbled it all the way to score against Verona.
- The moment when Ibrahimovich scored a wonder of a goal against England.
- The moment when Diego Maradona dribbled through England's defense at the 1986 World Cup to score one of the greatest goals of all time.

I define the moment of magic as that moment in time when a trained skill meets opportunity. You too can experience such moments in your life and business. The moment of magic occurs for you when you can apply a skill that you have burned into your subconscious mind through constant practice and repetition to an opportunity that presents itself. This is why Maldini believes he and his teammates can play now how they did many years ago—and you can get there too.

.

4 EVERY TEAM HAS A GAME-WINNING PLAN UNTIL …

Whenever you are going through life's challenges, remember that for iron to be cast into its desired form, it must first go through intense heat.

Every team has a game-winning plan—until they concede an early goal. In the 2017 FA Cup Final game between Chelsea and Arsenal, the odds were against Arsenal: Chelsea had just finished the season as premier league champions, and Arsenal were finishing off a bad season by its own standards. The bookmakers picked Chelsea as the overwhelming favorite to win the game—but the results proved otherwise.

Arsenal scored in the fourth minute, and it totally threw the Chelsea team off its stride. The contentious nature in which the goal was scored also added to the disruption of the Chelsea team. Alexis Sánchez appeared to have handled the ball before running on to his own flick and then putting the ball past Thibaut Courtois and into the goal. The manner in which the Chelsea team lost composure after that goal shows the power of an early goal.

A lot of preparation goes into each game. Before a game, there are scouting reports, endless drills, tactical updates, video reviews, and multiple practice sessions. Each player walks on the pitch with a set of instructions and an exact plan of what he must do once the game begins.

An early goal conceded in the first five minutes of a game, for example, can completely change the team's original plan for the game. I had something similar happen to one of my teams. I was a volunteer coach of a youth soccer team, and we were two games away from an undefeated season. We had won all our previous games, except for one against a really good team, with whom we had tied. Before playing the team for the second time in the season, I had worked with my team on a winning game plan.

At the beginning of the game, every one of my players knew what the plan was and they were ready to put it into action. The referee blew the whistle, and away we went. Barely two minutes into the game, the referee blew his whistle, calling a foul against my team. The other team was awarded a penalty kick, on which they scored.

The early goal completely disrupted my team's plan, creating uncertainty and nervousness among my players. Instead of pushing for a winning goal, we were now chasing the game and trying to score an equalizing goal. The opposing team, on the other hand, had built up some confidence and a sense of security from their early goal. We ended up losing the game—our only loss of the season. I had a talk with my team at the end of the game letting them know that in soccer, things don't always go according to plan.

Just like in the game of soccer, people have plans, dreams, and goals for success in life and business. However, things do not always go according to plan.

A sudden loss, car trouble, a new hire doesn't work out, a contract gets canceled, financial trouble, and health issues are just some examples of unplanned setbacks that can throw your plans into disarray and knock you off your game.

In the face of setbacks, you'll always be tempted to give up. My advice? Stay in the game, keep the end goal in sight, and let your will to win be stronger than your setbacks. An "early goal conceded" does not mean the game is over. It just means that you have to adjust your game plan. There is still "time on the clock," and you still have plenty to play for.

5 EMOTIONAL CONTROL

*Image is what everyone sees when the lights are on; character is
what remains when the lights are off.*

José Mourinho is one of the most successful coaches
in history. He is loved by many and hated by just as
many. There is one thing about him, however, that no
one can deny: He is a winner.

Mourinho has coached some of the biggest clubs in
the world, namely Porto, Chelsea, Inter Milan, Real
Madrid, and Manchester United. At each of these
clubs, he has won important titles, such as the
Champions League and League Titles. He has also
been a part of some of the biggest derbies in world
football, including:

- O Classico: FC Porto and Benfica Derby in Portugal
- London Derby: Chelsea and Arsenal Derby in England
- El Classico: Real Madrid and Barcelona Derby in Spain
- Milan Derby: Inter Milan and AC Milan Derby in Italy
- Manchester Derby: Manchester United and Manchester City Derby in England

These high-octane games are emotionally charged. Beyond the game, the pride of the players and that of the fans is at stake, and no one wants to lose. In one after-game interview, Mourinho said something that caught my attention. He said that in all the derbies he had been a part of, before each game, he always talked to his players about emotional control. He said, "To win derbies, you need emotional control."

It is so easy for a player to get carried away by the significance of a game that he loses his head, makes bad decisions, and lets his team down. Many players have lost control in high-profile games, one of the most famous being Zinedine Zidane, when he head-butted an opposing player in the 2006 World Cup Final game between France and Italy. Zidane's moment of madness was provoked by a verbal exchange he had with Italy defender Marco Materazzi. Zidane was sent off and Italy went on to lift the trophy.

It is important that players maintain emotional control during these fiercely competitive games. To be the best, they must focus on the task at hand and not get distracted by the magnitude of the occasion.

Similarly, I believe it is important in our personal lives and in the business world to maintain some form of emotional control. In fact, emotional control is a trait I look for when considering hiring or promoting an employee to a position of authority. If a person does not excel in this area, I question their leadership ability—I value emotional control that highly.

It is important to learn how to control your emotions so that you don't end up doing something you will regret. Some actions, once taken, can prove to be costly. These actions cannot be taken back, and even when you apologize, the impact still lingers. For example, we see this with companies whose sales continue to decline even after apologizing for a negative remark made by a member of the executive team.

Of course, certain situations evoke emotions that are difficult to overcome. These emotions can overpower our thoughts and make us act in ways we ordinarily wouldn't. Rather than being overpowered by your emotions, however, it is important that you keep the end goal in sight and constantly work on developing your emotional muscle. A well-developed emotional muscle will guide your decision-making process and build your character to get you through tough situations.

6 IT IS A TEAM SPORT

He who masters the power formed by a group of people working together has within his grasp one of the greatest powers known to man.

Earlier in the book, I mentioned that there are two reasons why soccer is the biggest sport in the world. In the first chapter, we discussed the first reason, which is "All you need is a ball." The second reason is this: Soccer is a team sport. You need other players to play the game of soccer, and this appeals to who we are by nature.

Human beings are social creatures. The idea that life will be fine if we go through it alone is misleading. The truth is that we need and long for the company of others. The inherent sense of belonging to a group or community means it's important for us to be accepted by the group; we do whatever we can to earn its acceptance, and when we do, we feel loved and enjoy our interactions with other members. Being in such a group becomes part of our identity, and we take immense pride in our association with it. We identify ourselves by the group to which we belong.

A tight community of people is one of the few things that can provide the feelings we seek internally. That is why people long so much to be a part of a group that may offer what they feel is missing in their lives. We feel safe in the numbers that the group or community has to offer us. We feel that when more people are involved in the group, we have more people to support us when we need it. We also feel protected and content with the knowledge that someone else out there cares about us and is willing to look after our interests. In fact, the whole idea of social media is built on our need to connect and interact with others.

From my experience over the years, I can honestly say that superior success in business is a team sport. You will achieve more with a committed and focused team driving toward the same results than you would by yourself. High-performing teams also require a leadership figure to help drive performance. Without a leader, there is often a lack of direction and order within the group.

Every great leader has certain qualities that set them apart. For one, relationship building is a big part of being a leader. Forming strong bonds with people around you is essential to your success. To strengthen your position as a leader, you have to know everyone's likes, dislikes, needs, hopes, and dreams. Great leaders know how to get everyone working together, irrespective of differences. They help others put their differences aside so they don't get in the way of the group's common goal.

Great leaders know how to not only determine the mood of those around them but also calibrate the people around them to the right mood level. This is done through effective communication and by developing a deep understanding of those who are on your team. When they are sad, for example, you know what to say or do to make them happy again. A good leader uses this to keep individuals around him motivated and performing at their best.

A great leader is also a good judge of ability. He knows what each person is capable of, so when he sees people not performing to the best of their abilities, he can step in to make the necessary adjustments. A great leader can also match people to their strengths so they always perform at their best. If a great leader spots weaknesses, he can work with the person to turn those weaknesses into strengths.

A great leader inspires alignment and commitment from others, getting everyone focused and working toward the same cause. Together, as a force, everyone is better positioned to achieve the objectives. A leader does this by clearly communicating the cause and helping everyone involved understand the required commitment.

Being a great leader doesn't require that you know everything there is to know. It does, however, require that you surround yourself with the right people who can make up for whatever it is you lack. If you lack knowledge, expertise, or abilities in certain areas, you should have certain people you can go to for help. A great leader is also a student of learning. He is committed to improvement and is constantly working toward it.

7 LEADERSHIP IN SEVEN WORDS

There is a need to focus on training the people in leadership. As corporations promote through the ranks, what you end up with is managers in leadership positions. They are great at managing processes but know nothing about managing people.

Part of the work I do as a consultant involves training and developing leaders. What I have realized over the years is that good leaders are vital to the success of the places they serve. If you look at anything successful, you will see traces of a good leader in it. Conversely, when good leadership is absent, it is clear to see.

"A leader is a steward of trust" is a powerful truth about leadership. I discovered this truth while observing the game of soccer. In a typical soccer club, there are many layers of leadership. There is the coach, the owner of the team, the board of directors, the club captain, and more. Let's focus on the team coach.

A team coach is hired because those who've hired him have put their trust in him to coach and lead the team. It doesn't stop there. The players put their trust in the coach to lead them in the right direction; the fans put their trust in the coach to lead the team to success; the team's owner and the board of directors put their trust in the coach to achieve the objectives they have set for him; and the assistant coach and the backroom staff all put their trust in the coach to lead them down the right path.

These people collectively trust that the coach will make the right decisions and put out the best team that can win on game day. They also trust that the coach will keep the team's best interests at heart.

As a steward of trust, a leader is responsible for the trust that others have given him. When a team coach understands this, he takes actions that are consistent with that understanding and great measures to not betray the trust given by the team's owner, the board of directors, the club captain, the fans, the players, and the backroom staff. The team coach makes sure that everything he does reflects this level of trust.

The statement "A leader is a steward of trust" is as true in the game of soccer as it is in any form of leadership. It is the same in business, in school, in government, in every household, or anywhere a leader serves. A leader's job is to protect the trust his supporters have placed in him. The leader accomplishes this by acting according to the expectations of this trust. When a leader understands that he is a steward of trust, he understands the bulk of what leadership is about.

Everything a leader does—a leader's thoughts, plans, and actions—should be built on this core principle. A leader should allow this principle to be his guide as he embarks on the journey of leadership. When a leader does this, he sees much success.

8 "IT IS IMPOSSIBLE"

What is considered impossible is someone else's opinion. What is possible is my decision.

Up until 2017, many said that it was impossible for a team to win the UEFA Champions League two seasons in a row. They had plenty of reason for saying so. The Champions League is the world's preeminent club cup competition. Forget just winning it once—it is tough to even qualify to play in it. To qualify, a club must finish the previous season in one of the top spots in its domestic league, or teams could earn a wild card by playing through and winning the Europa League competition.

For many years, the belief that it was impossible to win two seasons in a row held strong. The evidence lay in the fact that it had never been done in the modern era. Many teams had tried; they would come close but failed. The failure of those teams continued to back the belief that it was impossible to do. People would say, "If that team, as good as they are, couldn't do it, that goes to show you that it must be impossible."

In 2017, that all changed: Real Madrid became the first team to win it twice in a row. Once they did, it made front-page news all around the world. The impossible was made possible. Achieving that feat was great enough, but the team did not stop there. In 2018, Real Madrid won it again for a record three times in a row. What was once impossible was made possible all over again.

How many times in your life have you been told that something was impossible or could not be done? We've all heard it at some point. But what we do with what we are told is up to us. We can choose to believe it and accept it as truth, or we can choose not to believe it. If we accept it as truth, we feel powerless over the situation; if we choose not to accept it, though, then we can do something about it.

One of the biggest battles we must fight on our way to success is that which exists in our heads. This battle has to do with what we believe and how we interpret what is in front of us. Your belief system today is not something that you developed overnight. It's been shaped over time, based on the various life experiences you've had, starting from childhood. These experiences have limited, developed, or strengthened your belief system. Just like computers work with an operating system, humans work with a set of beliefs too. Your belief system shapes the way you think and, ultimately, the actions you take.

Teams and organizations also work from a set of beliefs that drive employee behavior and the organizations' operations. In the case of Real Madrid, the team's belief system resulted in winning the competition twice in a row. Even though no other team had done it before, this team believed that it was the team to do it. After winning the second time, the team's success reaffirmed their belief. This strengthened belief made it easier for them to go for the third win.

You too can program your belief system to work to

your advantage by having a "can do" attitude and not a "this is impossible" attitude. When you encounter a challenging situation, notice the difference when you face it with a "can do" attitude as opposed to a "this is impossible" attitude. Say to yourself, "I can do this. I have what it takes." As you repeat this to yourself over time, you will feel a change inside you, and the thing that looked almost too challenging to overcome before no longer will. You feel different about yourself and be more willing to take on the challenge.

We all have dreams, goals, and aspirations in life, but having a strong belief system by which you can achieve them plays a big part in realizing those dreams. Whether you know it or not, every time you make a choice, you are literally deciding what your beliefs should be. Recognize the power lies within you to develop the right belief system—the type that will empower you to take on your dreams, goals, and aspirations. If you believe it is possible, you are already one step closer to achieving it.

9 POSITIONING FOR SUCCESS

*Mountains are only a problem when they are bigger than you.
You should develop yourself so much that you become bigger
than the mountains you face.*

In its simplest terms, the object of the game of soccer
is to score more goals in your opponent's goal than
your opponent scores in yours. The more times a
team outscores their opponent, the more games they
win and the more they are considered successful.
Success in soccer is therefore tied to scoring goals.

Each team has eleven players who play in four
different positions on the field: goalkeeper, defenders,
midfielders, and forwards. Of all the positions, the
forwards usually score most of the team's goals or are,

at least, expected to. I'm emphasizing the word "expected" because there are exceptions to that rule. There are situations where you have a good midfielder or a player in a different position who outscores the forwards. For the most part, however, the forwards are supposed to be the highest-scoring players on the team.

So why do the forwards score more goals or are expected to score more goals than the rest of the team? The easy answer that you would get from most people is that it is because it is their job to do so. That's true, but there's a lot more to it.

The biggest reason the forwards outscore or are expected to outscore the others on their team is because the forwards spend the most time farthest up the pitch. They are also closer to the opponent's goal during the game than any other player on their team. For this reason, they have more of an opportunity to score goals because of their field position. The key word here is opportunity. Proximity to opportunity is why forwards have more chances to score more goals than a goalkeeper, a defender, or a midfielder.

If you line up a million goalkeepers, a million

defenders, and a million forwards, you will notice a pattern within each group of players. Goalkeepers are usually the least skillful with their feet. There are exceptional talents out there and certain goalkeepers that stand out from the rest, but for the most part, this is the case. Defenders are usually better with their feet and more skillful than goalkeepers. Once again, this is the rule, although there are exceptions.

Farther up the field, you will find that midfielders and forwards are usually better than defenders and goalkeepers with the ball. The distinction in terms of ability, however, blurs between midfielders and forwards. Their ability with the ball becomes interchangeable; you will find forwards who are better with the ball than midfielders and midfielders who are better with the ball than forwards.

You will also notice that goalkeepers on the whole score the fewest goals on the team. Defenders generally score more goals than goalkeepers, and midfielders generally score more goals than defenders. For midfielders and forwards, it is, again, interchangeable.

Here is what it means and how it all ties back to

success in life. Let's assume that, as you grow in education, skills, and talent, the farther up the field you go. To make it easy to follow, we will say that a person who is in a "goalkeeper position" in life, for example, has the least amount of education, skills, and talent. If we use goal scoring as a measure of success, then we can say that a person in the "goalkeeper position" is the least successful because they score the fewest goals.

Moving up the field, a person who is in a "defender position" in life has more education, skills, and talent than the person who is in the "goalkeeper position." Also using goal scoring as a measure of success, we can say that people in the "defender position" in life are more successful than those in the "goalkeeper position" because defenders generally score more goals than goalkeepers.

Moving up the field another level, a person who is in a "midfielder position" in life has more education, skills, and talent than the person who is in a "defender position." Using goal scoring as a measure of success, we can say people in the "midfielder position" in life are more successful than those in the "defender position" because midfielders, on the whole, score more goals than defenders.

The distinction in education, skills, and talent is, however, blurred between midfielders and forwards. You will also realize that their goal scoring ability is interchangeable. There are many midfielders who score more goals than forwards as well as forwards who score more than midfielders.

The reason for this is because there is an imaginary line that separates goalkeepers and defenders from midfielders and forwards. I call this the "enough line." Once you cross the enough line, your chance of success goes up tremendously. The enough line is important because it tells us a few things:

- You do not have to be the most educated person in the world to be successful; you just have to be educated *enough*.
- You do not have to be the most skilled person in the world to be successful; you just have to be skilled *enough*.
- You do not have to be the most talented person in the world to be successful; you just have to be talented *enough*.

Any player on the field is capable of scoring goals. Goalkeepers score, and defenders do too. What matters most is that you are on the field in a position and playing the game. Being on the field gives you an opportunity to score. To increase your chances of scoring, you need to progress toward the "enough line." You do this by developing yourself in the areas you want to strengthen. One thing is for sure: You will not score any goals sitting on the reserve bench. No player does. You will only score if you are on the field playing. Get in the game, grow yourself, and start "scoring" for your success.

10 CAN I HAVE YOUR JERSEY?

Even though our time in this life is temporary, if we live well enough, our legacy will last forever.

One longtime tradition among players is to swap jerseys after a game. This is when players literally remove the game jerseys from their body and swap it with a player on the opposing team.

The jersey swap is symbolic in many ways. For some, it is a show of friendship and goodwill; for others, it is a show of respect or just a way to mark the occasion.

Many of the most popular players in the world sometimes have a line of players competing to be the first to swap jerseys with them after a game. Players who successfully swap jerseys with them triumphantly walk away with a memento in hand. The jersey they collect becomes a symbol of the occasion to be remembered for a long time.

Most players who exchange jerseys can easily afford to go to the store to purchase a replica jersey of the one they just received. However, purchasing a jersey is not the same as having one off the back of someone you admire. Walking away with a worn jersey of a player with whom you shared the same field carries a more significance.

Exchanging a jersey with a player you admire says "I like what you have done in the sport, and it is an honor to have your jersey." The players whose shirts are in the highest demand are often the best players— those who have thrilled and created great memories for both other players and fans of the sport. For this reason, it is a show of respect to ask for their jersey as they walk off the field.

Life is like a soccer field. As we go through it, we run

and we stop. We have victories and we have losses. We fall down and we get back up. One day, the referee who represents a higher power up above will blow the final whistle, and it will all be over. When the whistle blows, it will be time to step off the field.

As you walk off the field, will anyone ask you for your jersey? Will your children, your friends, your spouse, your grandchildren, or other family members ask you for it? Will your coworkers and business associates be proud to put your jersey on? Will they proudly wear your name across their back?

What will your legacy be when you walk off this field? Will it be strong enough to bring back great memories of your playing days? What difference will you have made in the world? How many lives will you have impacted? How many people will be better off because they knew you?

What will people say about you when your playing days are over? Will they say that you were the type of player that gave your very best? Will they say that you lived as the very best version of yourself? These are some questions you need to ask yourself about the legacy you are going to leave behind.

While you are still here on the field of life with time left on the clock, you have the opportunity to write your story. I encourage you to write it in the way that you want it to be told—a way that will make you proud. I also encourage you to write your story in a way that will encourage others to wear your jersey proudly with your name across their back.

Also get this bestseller from the Author:

Wealth for All: Living a Life of Success at the Edge of Your Ability

ABOUT THE AUTHOR

Idowu Koyenikan is a highly quoted author and internationally recognized business consultant. He helps individuals and organizations break through to new levels. As an expert contributor, he has been featured in media outlets such as the Harvard Business Review, Forbes, Yahoo, BBC, MSN, ABC, Chicago Tribune, Huffington Post, Nasdaq, Boston Globe and many more. Idowu is a volunteer soccer coach at his local YMCA where he helps young boys and girls prepare for life through the game of soccer.

Tell us your success story

Was this book helpful to you in any way? We would like to hear the impact this book has on your life. You can also connect with Idowu Koyenikan, the author of this book, through any of the channels below:

Website: www.IkElevates.com
E-mail: IkElevates@gmail.com
Twitter Handle: @IkElevates
Facebook Page: Idowu Koyenikan
YouTube: IkElevates
Instagram: Idowu Koyenikan

Made in the USA
Columbia, SC
30 October 2018